Jesus Loves Me:

this I know for the Bible tells me so

Easter Coloring Book

ISBN: 9781798577257

Images used are public domain, or from supercoloring.com. Images used with permission under the creative commons share-alike 4.0 international license as listed below:

Images on pages 3, 59, 73, 77 by Lena London.
Image on page 21 by Natalia Moskovina.

This coloring book tells the story of Jesus Christ's final weeks on earth, from the Triumphal Entry to His Ascension.
It is a summary of the events recorded in the Holy Bible.

To read these Bible stories for yourself, please search the New Testament books below:
 Matthew chapters 20 - 28
 Mark chapters 11 - 16
 Luke chapters 19 - 24
 John chapters 12 - 20

We love because He first loved us.

John 4:19

Jesus and His disciples traveled to Jerusalem to celebrate the spring Jewish holy days.

As they approached Jerusalem, Jesus sent two of His disciples to a nearby village to fetch a donkey with its foal. "If anyone asks why you are taking them," Jesus told the men, "say the Lord has need of them, and they will allow you to have them".
So the disciples did as Jesus instructed.

The disciples brought the animals to Jesus and spread their coats on them.
Jesus sat on the donkey and rode it into Jerusalem.

Many people recognized Jesus and His disciples.
The crowd spread coats on the road before
Jesus.
Some people cut palm branches from the trees
and spread them on the road along with the
coats.
Others waved the branches as Jesus passed by.

The crowd called out greetings to Jesus.

They shouted "Hosanna to the Son of David!" and "Blessed is He who comes in the name of the Most High!"

They welcomed Jesus as their promised Savior and King.

When Jesus arrived at the Temple in Jerusalem
He was very angry with what He saw.
People were buying, selling and conducting
business as if the Temple was a marketplace.

Jesus threw out the vendors and overturned the
money-changers tables.
He scolded them for their disrespectful behavior
in the Temple, God's holy house.

Jesus knew He had only a few days left to live on earth. He spent these days teaching.

Jesus spent time with His disciples preparing them to take over His ministry.

Jesus tried to make them understand the meaning and purpose of His upcoming death. He told them they would not understand some of what He was saying until later.

Jesus promised that He would one day return to earth to take all those who believe in Him to live with Him in His eternal kingdom.

Every morning Jesus went to the Temple courts to teach. Crowds of people came to hear Him speak. Many of His teachings were given through stories called parables.

As Jesus taught at the Temple, the Jewish elders, Sadducees and Pharisees questioned Him.
They did not like Jesus teaching the people.
These leaders believed they were the experts on Jewish law and history.

These men were so angry they planned to have Jesus arrested.

Jesus visited with His friends Mary, Martha and Lazarus.

Mary poured an expensive bottle of perfume on Jesus. Jesus praised Mary for what she had done. She had anointed Jesus, preparing Him for His death.

But Judas, the disciple who was in charge of the money, scolded her. Judas thought this was wasteful. The perfume was expensive and could have been sold for a large sum of money - to help the poor.

Judas went to the Jewish leaders and offered to help them arrest Jesus. They paid Judas 30 pieces of silver coins for the betrayal of his friend.

The day before Passover was a busy day.
It was called Preparation Day.
The lambs were killed and prepared for the
Passover meal that evening.

The Jews also had to prepare for the week-long
Feast of Unleavened Bread, which began the
following day. All yeast and yeast products had to
be removed from their homes.

The first and last days of this feast were special
holy days, or Sabbaths –so no work was allowed.

Jesus asked His disciples to prepare a Passover meal. He looked forward to sharing this special feast with them.

That evening, before they ate, Jesus washed His disciples' feet.
The washing of feet was an example for the disciples - to be servants to others, to go beyond what was expected.
It was also symbolic of the washing away of sins, which Jesus would do with His death on the cross.

As they were eating, Jesus took the bread, broke it and gave it to the disciples to eat.

He said, "take it, this is my body which is given for you".

Then after the meal Jesus took a cup of wine and held it up. This cup was called the cup of redemption.

He declared the wine was the sign of a new covenant.

The wine represented His blood which would be poured out (spilled) for the forgiveness of sins.

He told His disciples to remember Him when they ate the bread and drank the wine.

After the Passover meal was finished, Jesus told His disciples that one of them would betray Him. They looked around in disbelief – how could one of them do such a terrible thing?

Jesus knew the evil plan Judas had made with the Jewish leaders - that Judas would betray Him for 30 pieces of silver.
Jesus now excused Judas from the table. Jesus told Judas "What you are doing, do quickly".

Judas had arranged a signal to notify the Roman soldiers who to arrest. Judas would greet Jesus with a kiss. It was not unusual to greet friends with a kiss at this time. This 'secret' signal was a way Judas could betray Jesus without the others knowing he was the one responsible.

After Judas left, Jesus continued speaking with the eleven remaining disciples. He told them He would be leaving them soon, but promised to send a helper – the Holy Spirit, to them.

Jesus surprised them when He told them that they would deny knowing Him.
Peter, certain he would stay beside Jesus no matter what trials came, refused to believe it.
Jesus told him, "Peter, tonight - before the rooster crows to welcome the morning, you will have denied knowing me three times".

After they sang a hymn, Jesus and His disciples walked to the Mount of Olives.
There was a garden area there called the Garden of Gethsemane.
Jesus and His disciples went into this garden.

Jesus asked His disciples to keep watch and walked a short distance away to be alone.

He prayed to His Father in heaven. He prayed for His disciples, He prayed for all believers, and He prayed for Himself.

Jesus walked over to check on His disciples three times, and each time they had fallen asleep.
Jesus was alone in His sorrow.

Jesus' sweat fell like drops of blood as He pleaded for the burden of suffering and death to be removed.
Finally He said "not my will, but Yours be done".
He accepted His task to die for man's sin.
An angel came and cared for Jesus in the garden.

When Jesus had finished praying He walked over to His disciples and said, "now, let us go for the time is near".

It was dark. A large group of Roman soldiers and other men arrived, carrying torches, clubs, and swords. With them were Judas and the high priests' servant, Malchus.

Judas stepped forward and greeted Jesus with a kiss - the pre-arranged signal of betrayal. Immediately the soldiers moved to arrest Jesus.

Peter grabbed a sword and cut off Malcus'
right ear.
Jesus told Peter to put away his sword.

Jesus assured the disciples that if He asked,
many angels would come to protect Him.
Jesus was allowing Himself to be arrested, so
that God's plan for His life and man's
salvation could be complete.

Jesus healed Malchus' ear.

The soldiers brought Jesus first to the priest Annas' house, then to the high priest, Caiaphas' house.
Jesus was mocked, beaten, and questioned in an illegal trial.

The disciples Peter and John had followed Jesus and the soldiers at a distance.
They now waited to see what would happen.

Peter remained in the outer courtyard and warmed himself by the fire.

As he waited, some people questioned whether Peter was a friend of Jesus.
Twice Peter answered "No, I don't know the man."

Later, just before sunrise, Peter was again recognized as one of Jesus' followers.

For the third time Peter denied knowing Jesus.

Immediately the rooster crowed.
When he heard the rooster Peter remembered
what Jesus had said, and he wept.

As it was now morning, the chief priests had Jesus tied up and brought to the Roman governor, Pontius Pilate.

The Jewish leaders waited outside while Jesus was brought inside the building. They did not go in themselves - they wanted to remain ceremonially clean for the Passover celebration that evening.

After questioning Jesus, Pilate could find no reason to kill Him.

Pilate went out to speak with the Jewish leaders. They insisted Jesus had committed a crime worthy of death.

41

Pilate had promised the Jews that he would release a prisoner for the festival.
Pilate offered them a choice between Jesus and a murderer named Barabbas.
The people shouted for Barabbas to be released.

They demanded Jesus be crucified.
"Crucify! Crucify him!" they shouted.

Pilate reluctantly agreed, but washed his hands of any wrongdoing.
He handed Jesus over to the soldiers.

The Roman soldiers placed a crown of thorns on Jesus' head, beat Him and spit on Him.

43

Carrying His cross, Jesus was led to a hill outside Jerusalem called Golgotha, which means 'Place of the Skull'.

When Jesus fell under its heavy load, a man named Simon the Cyrene was made to carry the cross.

A large crowd of people followed, mourning and crying.

45

It was still morning, around 9 am, when the soldiers nailed Jesus' hands and feet to the wooden cross.

He was hung between two other men, both criminals.

A sign ordered by Pontius Pilate was hung above Jesus' head. It had the crime for which Jesus was being punished written on it.

The sign stated 'King of the Jews' in three languages – Hebrew, Greek, Aramaic - so all who passed by could read it.

The Roman soldiers stood guard nearby and divided Jesus' clothes among them.
They cast lots for His tunic which was woven in one piece, and they did not want to tear it.

Standing nearby were Jesus' mother, Mary Magdalene, and His disciples. Seeing John, Jesus asked him to care for His mother, Mary.

A crowd had gathered to watch the crucifixions. The people called to Jesus "prove you are truly God - come down from the cross and save yourself". Even one of the criminals who hung beside Jesus began to mock Him.

The other criminal told him to stop. He knew they were being punished for a crime they had done, but Jesus was an innocent man.
He asked Jesus to "remember him when He entered His kingdom".
Jesus told this man that he would be with Him in paradise.

Darkness covered the land from 12 noon until 3pm. Around three in the afternoon Jesus cried out "my God, my God why have you forsaken me?"
He was offered sour wine on a sponge to drink.

Jesus cried out "It is finished" and gave up His spirit. Jesus Christ was dead.

Immediately the Temple curtain (veil) which covered the Most Holy Place tore in half, from top to bottom.

An earthquake shook the land, and tombs were opened. Dead people came alive and went into the city where many people saw them.

The Roman centurion and others who were keeping watch over the crucifixions saw these events and were terrified. "Surely He was the Son of God" they said.

Because it was almost evening - which would be the start of a holy day, called a 'high' Sabbath, the Jews were anxious to get the men off the crosses.

It was the Roman soldiers' duty to made sure the men were dead. One way to hasten death was to break the criminals legs.

When the soldiers came to Jesus, He appeared to be already dead. Instead of breaking His legs, they pierced His side with a spear.

Satisfied Jesus really was dead, they lowered His body off the cross.

A rich man named Joseph, who was secretly a follower of Christ, went to Pilate to ask for Jesus' body. Pilate gave Joseph permission to bury Jesus.

Joseph bought an expensive linen cloth to wrap Jesus' body in, and a man named Nicodemus brought spices of myrrh and aloe.
Jesus' body was prepared for burial.
They laid Him in the new tomb owned by Joseph, and rolled a large stone over, to block the entrance.

Mary Magdalene and Mary the mother of Joses were there, watching.

The Jewish elders and priests had heard rumors that Jesus would rise from the dead after three days and three nights.

They asked Pilate to send Roman soldiers to guard the entrance of Jesus' tomb.
These leaders believed Jesus' disciples were going to steal His body from the grave, and so pretend Jesus had risen from the dead.

Two Roman soldiers were placed outside the tomb to guard it.
The guards were to make certain Jesus' body remained inside the tomb.

The Sabbath days of rest passed.
Early in the morning, on the first day of the week, Mary Magdalene, Mary the mother of James, and Salome went to Jesus' tomb. They brought with them prepared spices and perfumes to anoint Jesus.

When the women arrived at the tomb, they saw the stone covering the doorway had been rolled away.
The Roman guards appeared to be asleep.
Two men dressed in white were at the tomb.
These angels told the women that Jesus was not there, He was alive and would soon visit the disciples.

The women went back to the believers who were gathered together, mourning Christ's death.
When they told the believers what they had seen and heard, Peter and John raced to the tomb - they had to see this for themselves!

When the men arrived at the tomb, it was empty, just as the women had said.

A little while later, Mary Magdalene was outside the tomb, crying.
The angels asked her why she was so upset.
She answered, "They have taken my Master and I don't know where He is".

Just then a man came over and asked her who she was looking for. Mary thought this man was the gardener, until He spoke her name, "Mary".
Surprised and delighted, Mary called out "Rabboni!" which means "Teacher".

Jesus told Mary not to touch Him as He had not yet ascended to His Father.
He asked Mary to tell His disciples that she had seen Him alive.

Later this same day, two men were walking from Jerusalem to a village called Emmaus.
As they traveled they discussed all that had happened in Jerusalem over the past few days.

While they were talking, Jesus joined them, but God prevented these men from recognizing Jesus. On their journey, Jesus taught the men the scriptures - about Moses, the prophets, and about His death and resurrection.

When they arrived in Emmaus the men asked Jesus to stay with them for it was getting late - it was almost evening.
As they sat to eat, Jesus took the bread, blessed it, broke it apart and gave it to them. At this moment God allowed the men to recognize Jesus was the man sitting with them.
Then Jesus disappeared.

The men returned to Jerusalem that evening to tell the disciples what they had experienced.

That evening most of Jesus' disciples were together in a locked room.
They had locked the door because they were afraid the Jews who had wanted Jesus dead would come looking for them too.

Suddenly Jesus appeared before them and said to them "peace be with you".
Jesus showed them His pierced hands and side.

The disciples were overjoyed to see Jesus.
Jesus told them to remain in Jerusalem until He sent them the gift of the Holy Spirit.
He told them to carry on His message, to preach the good news of His death and resurrection.

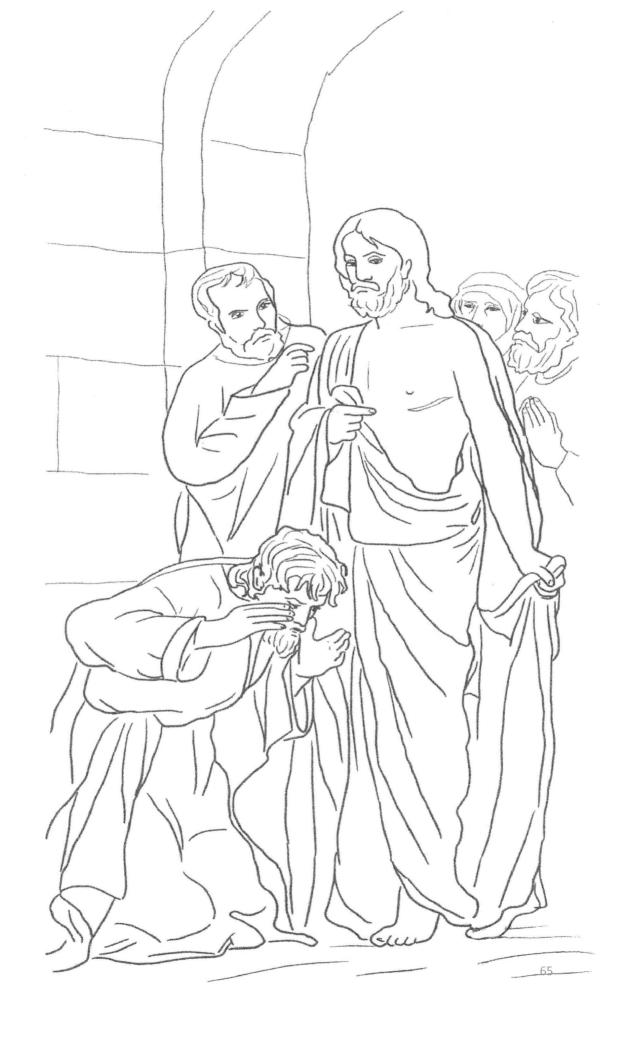

Thomas, one of the twelve, was not in the room when Jesus had appeared to the disciples. He refused to believe Jesus was alive until he could see and touch Jesus for himself.

One week later, as they were gathered together in a locked room, Jesus appeared before the disciples again. This time Thomas was present. He saw and touched the holes in Jesus' body and believed.

Jesus told him, "Blessed are those who have not seen Me, and still believe".

Jesus and His disciples walked a short distance outside Jerusalem.
Once they were near Bethany, Jesus lifted up His hands and blessed His disciples.
He told them "Go into all the world and preach the gospel. Whoever believes and is baptized will be saved, but whoever does not believe will be condemned."

After saying these words, the Lord Jesus was taken up into heaven.
This is called the Ascension of Jesus.

The disciples worshipped God, and returned to Jerusalem with great joy.
There they waited for the promised gift of the Holy Spirit.

For whoever calls on the name of the Lord shall be saved.

Romans 10:13

So whether you eat or drink or whatever you do, do it all for the glory of God

Corinthians 10:31

Be the first to hear of future book releases!

Subscribe to the "Wildrose Media" newsletter by submitting
your name and email address to:

www.wildrose-media.com

Additional books by Wildrose Media:
(visit our website, it will take you to our complete book selection on Amazon)

Journals and Notebooks by Wildrose Media:
Fun with Frames: Art Journal for Kids
Create Your Own Comic Book Vol. 1,2,3- classic 7" x 10" and XL size 8.5" x 11"
All About Me: Creative Writing Journal for Kids age 5-8
Draw Me a Story: Art Journal for Kids
Sermon Notebooks - various cover styles and sizes
Sunday School Notebooks for Kids
Daily Planner- undated pages
Fitness and Weight Loss Journal: A 90-Day Tracker
Songwriting Journal for Kids
Travel Journal for Kids

Children's Coloring Books:
The Birth of Jesus Christmas Coloring Book
A Vintage Christmas Coloring Book
Christmas Coloring Book
Easter Coloring and Activity Book
Easter Coloring Book

Christmas Devotional:
Love Came Down: Unwrapping the Gift of Our Risen Savior
        author - Janice Wilhelm

Printed in Great Britain
by Amazon